MW00652970

A

DELICATE

FIRE

THE STONEWALL INN BOOK SERIES:

THE NAME OF LOVE: *Classic Gay Love Poems* edited by
Michael Lassell

THE KEY TO EVERYTHING: *Classic Lesbian Love Poems*
edited by Gerry Gomez Pearlberg

IN YOUR EYES: *Quotations on Gay Love* edited by
Richard M. Derus

A DELICATE FIRE: *Quotations on Lesbian Love* edited by
Liz Tracey

A

DELICATE

FIRE

Quotations on Lesbian Love

EDITED AND WITH AN INTRODUCTION BY

Liz Tracey

A STONEWALL INN BOOK
ST. MARTIN'S PRESS ❧ NEW YORK

Design by Songhee Kim

Library of Congress Cataloging-in-Publication Data

A delicate fire : quotations on lesbian love / edited and with
   an introduction by Liz Tracey. — 1st ed.
      p.   cm.
   "A Stonewall Inn book."
   ISBN 0-312-14059-2
   1. Lesbianism—Quotations, maxims, etc.   I. Tracey, Liz.
HQ75.5.D47   1996
306.76'63—dc20   95-43461
                                             CIP

First Edition: February 1996

10 9 8 7 6 5 4 3 2 1

Excerpts from "Beautiful women", "Prayer to my Lady of Paphos"
and "The gods bless you" from *Sappho: A New Translation* by Mary
Barnard. Copyright © 1958 by the Regents of the University of
California; copyright renewed 1984 by Mary Barnard. Reprinted
by permission of the publisher.

To Alison

The argument could be made that what sets lesbians (as well as bisexual women) apart from their heterosexual counterparts is who they love. In fact, the entire history of the lesbian and gay liberation movement is founded on the cornerstone of love, no matter what conservatives or bigots say to the contrary. With that said, this book could be viewed as an acknowledgment of a struggle across the years to find that which is fulfilling in our lives: the good love of another woman.

I was surprised in putting this together at the seeming abundance of material, especially during times when we would have thought that love between women would have dared not speak its name, let alone publish itself in *Harper's Bazaar*. But there it was, and we should be made all the more glad for it.

The reader should understand that inclusion in this book does not necessarily say anything about the sexual orientation of the writer; many women writing at times when sexual freedom was nonexistent for them would probably not have identified themselves as lesbian in the post-queer, Gay 90s sense of the word. I have chosen to include writings that portray love between two women, regardless of who did the writing.

I must acknowledge debt to Keith Kahla, my editor, for the idea for this book; Victoria Sanders for her unending faith in my sometimes flagging spirit; the lesbian scholars whose research makes our lives richer; and Alison Shonkwiler, whose own love has restored my belief in the subject: This is my love letter to you.

A

DELICATE

FIRE

LOVE

An Overview

Entreat me not to leave you or to return from following you; for where you go I shall go, and where you lodge, I will lodge; your people shall be my people, and your God My God, where you die I will die, and there I shall be buried.

—THE BOOK OF RUTH, OLD TESTAMENT

"Love of woman for woman," what insane passion for unmitigated anguish and motherhood brought that into the mind?

—DJUNA BARNES, *Nightwood*

Come to me freely, and without reserve—with all your wants; with any complaints. I feel that I shall be quite fond of you.

—KATE CHOPIN, "The Falling in Love of Fedora: A Sketch"

Love is the only shocking act left on the face of the earth. Eroticism, murder, betrayal, starvation, torture, war, all pale in the face of love.

—SANDRA BERNHARD, *Love, Love and Love*

. . . I plead guilty
Of adoring you;
If you wish to punish me
That punishment will be my reward

—SOR JUANA INES DE LA CRUZ, "My Divine Lysi
(To the Marquise de la Laguna)"

A lot of strange things have been done in the name of love. In the search for love. And for the love of women. Crazy, silly, unreasonable things . . .

—ANN BANNON, *Journey to a Woman*

I don't believe in love at first sight. I'm not falling for you, but one step forward and you might fall for me.

—JEANETTE WINTERSON, *Art and Lies*

I have tried all means, Mathematical, Poetical, Statistical and Reasonable, to come to the Core of this Distemper known as Girls!

—DJUANA BARNES, *Ladies Almanack*

The love expressed between women is particular and powerful because we have had to love in order to live; love has been our survival.

—AUDRE LORDE in Mari Evans, ed., *Black Women Writers*

Are there many things in this cool-hearted world so utterly exquisite as the pure love of one woman for another?

—MARY MCLANE, *The Story of Mary McLane by Herself*

Looking at their faces: sweet, fine-featured, delicate, some of them; others coarse, sensual, heavily female. They all appealed to her, with their soft skirts, their clicking heels, their floating hair. . . .

God I love them, she thought to herself, vaguely surprised. I just love them. I love them all. I know I'm nuts, but I love them.

—ANN BANNON, *I am a Woman*

These Sapphists love women: friendship is never untinged with amorosity. . . .

—VIRGINIA WOOLF, diary entry

By Vulgar Eros long misled
I call'd thee Tyrant, mighty Love!
With idle fear my fancy fled
Nor ev'n thy pleasures wish'd to prove.

Condemned at length to wear thy chains,
Trembling I felt and ow'd thy might;
But soon I found my fears were vain,
Soon hugged my chain, and thought it light.

> —THE HONOURABLE SARAH PONSONBY, *The
> Ladies of Llangollen*

On occasion, when I fell in love, someone was
with me in the room and it was no longer empty,
but quickly, they became part of the furniture,
the television, the paint on the walls, and the
papers on my desk.

> —JANE DELYNN, *Don Juan in the Village*

I have this very bad habit of
Falling in love with the women
I'm sexually attracted to.
If I could just rid myself
of this vice,
I'm sure happiness would be
Just around the corner

— PAT CALIFIA, "The Femme Poem"

Life has prepared a soft bed for you
If gentle woman's love is yours.
You will not be robbed of it in later years,
For it rests not merely on beauty and assets.
However warm and abundant you are, however
    selfless,
In the same measure you will be paid back.

— MARIE VON NAJMAJAER, "Hymn to the
    Daughter of the Twentieth Century"

I love you. Those words were not worn out two thousand six hundred years ago. Are they worn out now? Perhaps, but not by repetition, but by strain. There are other ways of saying what I mean . . . Other words fit for the weight. Other words that pin me to an honesty I might not like. So much can be hidden in "I love you."

—JEANETTE WINTERSON, *Art and Lies*

There is so much beauty in being in love. . . .

—RADCLYFFE HALL, letter to Lady Una Troubridge

I am frightened. For I love you.

—JANET FLANNER, letter to Natalia Danesi Murray, *Darlinghissima*

The past does not worry me . . . I told you I was frightened of you. That's true. I don't want to fall in love with you all over again. . . . But if you really want me, I will come to you always, anywhere.

—VITA SACKVILLE-WEST, letter to Violet Trefusis, *Portrait of a Marriage*

"My little sweetheart," she says, bringing her face close enough for me to see the fine net of lines that carves her face into a weathered stone. "You love me, don't you little sweetheart, little lamb?"

Whether or not she listens anymore I am not sure, but I always answer yes: yes, I always say, yes I love you.

—BETH NUGENT, *City of Boys*

I remember seeing great statues of women in a park when I was small . . . and loving them. . . . I think I loved women even before that. . . . I think I always wanted to be loved by a woman . . . a woman like you. I can't imagine making love with a woman more beautiful than you.

—KATHERINE V. FORREST, *An Emergence of Green*

Love of Woman for Woman should increase Terror. I see that so far it does not. All is not as it should be!

—DJUNA BARNES, *Ladies Almanack*

These bunches of women living together, falling in love with each other because they haven't anyone else to fall in love with! It's obscene! Oh, take me away!

—MARION PATTON, *Dance on the Tortise*

Do not start. Do not blush. Let us admit in the privacy of our own society that these things sometimes happen. Sometimes women do like women.

—Virginia Woolf, *A Room of One's Own*

The rapport between ... two women can be absolute and perfect, as it can never be between man and woman, and perhaps some people just want this. . . .

—Claire Morgan (Patricia Highsmith), *The Price of Salt*

If Emma's bosom heav'd a pensive sigh,
The tear stood trembling in Elfrida's eye;
If pleasure gladdened her Elfrida's heart,
Still faithful Emma shar'd the larger part.

—A Lady, "Danebury; or the Power of Friendship" (1777)

She was in a hallucinatory state. It was too hot and her body could not get cool. Each part of her was sore and had a distinct odor. When Kate said "I love you," its effects lingered on Molly's skin like radiation. Molly could sail out the window on the strength of that alone.

—SARAH SCHULMAN, *People in Trouble*

Take this courage, my sisters, and show that you have as much right to exist and to love as the "normal" world! Defy this world and they will tolerate you, they will acknowledge you, and they will even envy you! Raise the weapons! You must and will succeed. I've done it. Why shouldn't you, every single one of you, succeed?

—ANONYMOUS "CONTRASEXUAL" (1901, Germany), translated by Lillian Faderman

Lesbos, where love is like the wild cascades
That throw themselves into the deepest gulfs,
And twist and run with gurglings and with
    sobs
Stormy and secret, swarming underground

— CHARLES BAUDELAIRE, "Lesbos"

I am sorry for you that you have loved me. You
might have been spared that at least, with better
luck . . .

— JANET FLANNER, letter to Natalia Danesi Murray,
Darlinghissima

Beautiful women,
my feelings for you
will never falter

— SAPPHO, "Beautiful women"

I love you with a love surpassing that of friendship. I go down on my knees to embrace you with all my heart.

—MADAME DE STAËL, *Passionate Exiles*

"I'm in love with you. . . . You don't seem surprised."

"I thought maybe you were," she said.

Tears began to run down my face. . . .

"I'm sorry."

"Me too," I said, dumbly.

—JANE DeLYNN, *Don Juan in the Village*

Love is difficult. Love gets harder, which is not the same as to say that it gets harder to love.

—JEANETTE WINTERSON, *The Poetics of Sex*

Let the dull world alone to talk and fight,
and with their vast ambitions nature fright;
Let them despise so innocent a flame,
While Envy, pride and faction play their game:
But we by Love sublim'd so high shall rise,
to pitty Kings, and Conquerors despise,
Since we that sacred union have engrost,
which they and all the sullen world have lost.

—KATHERINE FOWLER PHILIPS, "To Mrs. Mary
Awbrey" (1664)

Ah, how I love you, it paralyzes me—it makes
me heavy with emotion. . . . I tremble at the
thought of you—all day my whole being leans
out to you. . . . I dare not think of your arms.

—EVANGELINE MARS SIMPSON WHIPPLE, letter to
Rose Elizabeth Cleveland, *Odd Girls and Twilight
Lovers*

Ah, my friend! You do not know the ineffable delights, the exquisite pleasure, which arises from the union of affection and desire, when the whole soul and senses are abandoned to a lively imagination that renders every emotion delicate and rapturous.

—MARY WOLLSTONECRAFT, letter to Gilbert Imlay

You're the most universal lover I know. You're the moon that looks on many brooks.

—ALICE BROWN, *There and Here*

I assure you, with a love passing the Love of Men, that I am yours. . . .

—WILLIAM HAYLEY, *The Young Widow*

I love her with the seasons, with the winds,
As the stars worship, as anemones
Shudder in secret for the sun, as bees
Buzz round an open flower: in all kinds
My love is perfect; and in each she finds
Herself the goal

—"MICHAEL FIELD" (KATHERINE BRADLEY AND
EDITH COOPER), "Constancy"

People sometimes smile at the adoration of a
young girl for a woman, and there is no doubt
but that the feeling savours slightly of school
days and bread and butter. But there is also no
doubt that a girl who has once felt it has learned
what real love is, and that is no small lesson in
the book of life.

—ELLEN THORNEYCROFT FOWLER, *The
Farringdons*

I love my love with a dress and a hat
I love my love and not with this or with that
I love my love with a y because she is my
     bride
I love my love with a d because she is my love
     beside

—GERTRUDE STEIN, "Before the Flower of
     Friendship Faded Friendship Faded"

Sometimes I saw you in the bathroom, before
breakfast. You were always completely dressed.
You never left your room without being completely dressed. You came to the bathroom completely dressed and washed your face and brushed
your teeth in full uniform. Your shoes were
always polished.
You were always perfect.
I was in love with you.

—REBECCA BROWN, Bread

＊

Now is now. Now I'm here with you. No one else is here. No men, no parents. Just me. I love you. I love you more than I've ever loved anyone.

—JANE FUTCHER, *Past Lives*

＊

The most intense love of my life has come from a place I was taught not to expect or receive it.

—MELANIE HOPE, *Dare*

＊

Love in Man is Fear of Fear. Love in Women is Hope without Hope. Man fears all that can be taken from him, a Woman's Love includes that and then Lies down beside it. A Man's love is built to fit nature. A Woman's is a Kiss in the Mirror.

—DJUNA BARNES, *Ladies Almanack*

Manuela: I am so happy, so . . . so blissfully happy . . . because now, I know for certain—she loves me. She . . . opened her wardrobe . . . and took out a chemise . . . one of her own! . . . And gave it to me! I was to wear it and think of her. She didn't say that. . . . But she doesn't need to tell me anything. Her hand on my head tells me everything—sweet, good, dear white hand, that can hold so tenderly . . . Nothing can happen to me now—nothing in the whole world . . . She loves me! I know it—I feel it—it gives me strength . . . it makes me feel holy . . . From now on I will be quite different. I will have only good pure thoughts . . . and I will serve her . . . life has no other meaning . . .

—CHRISTA WINSLOE, *Mädchen in Uniform*, (film)
translated by Barbara Burnham

To see her is a Picture
To [hear] her is a Tune
To know her an Intemperance
As innocent as June

  —EMILY DICKINSON, "To see her is a Picture"

There are so many ways to love
and each way has its own delight—
Then be content to come to me
Only as spray the beating sea
Drives inland through the night.

    —SARA TEASDALE, "Spray"

One ought not to allow one's self the luxury of
losing one's head.

  —VITA SACKVILLE-WEST, letter, *Portrait of a
Marriage*

How does one fall in love? Do you trip? Do you stumble, lose your balance and drop to the sidewalk, graze your knee, graze your heart? Do you crash to the stony ground? Is there a precipice, from which you float, over the edge, forever?

—CATHLEEN SCHINE, *The Love Letter*

She thought of the old legends, of the knights who had to kill monsters before they could enjoy their love.

No demon here, thought Djuna, nothing but a woman drowning, who is clutching at me . . . I love her.

—ANAÏS NIN, *Cities of the Interior*

KISSING

Kiss my lips. She did.
Kiss my lips again she did.
Kiss my lips over and over and over again she
    did.

—GERTRUDE STEIN, "Lifting Belly"

Almost involuntarily, I drew her to me and kissed
her. The faintest flush tinged her cheek. I can't
describe how oddly she looked at me. . . . Then
I kissed her again.

—ALICE FRENCH, *My Lorelei*

Je t'embrasse avec amour et fidelité et passion.

—JANET FLANNER to Natalia Danesi Murray,
    Darlinghissima

My pale child, give me your mouth, and feed my own mad fires. How cool your red lips are. You haven't learned how love feels yet.

—MARIE-MADELEINE, "Sappho"

This morning I stopped the car on the long clear stretch and kissed her and she kissed me and on the way back from Nice too and when we got out of the car just now. . . . It was fun and I liked it.

—ERNEST HEMINGWAY, Catherine in *The Garden of Eden*

Lover to lover, no kiss,
no touch, but forever and ever this.

—H. D. (HILDA DOOLITTLE), "At Baia"

Even as a teenager Kate had never spent so much time kissing on the street as she did now, leaning into Molly's mouth against a parked car. She found her body pressed against all kinds of surfaces as these public kisses began to span seasons. There were barstools and doorways, bare patches of rare grass in a few scraggly parks.

—SARAH SCHULMAN, *People in Trouble*

. . . I opened my eyes and saw her face, suffused with passion, poised over me, her eyes heavy with desire, her face drawn thinner, longer with that desire, and her full rich lips reaching out to mine. I recognized this beloved face. My heart broke open with the profound, incontravertible knowledge that I had known and loved this woman for centuries.

—SKY VANDERLINDE, *Loving Blue*

Tell me it will be different this time.
No broken windows, no black eyes,
No jealous rages, no dirty dishes.
You don't even have to make it different.

Just tell me it will be
And I'll stay
As long as your kisses
can make me hope.

— PAT CALIFIA, "The Femme Poem"

She took my hands, and parted my fingers to
count the points as she told me why she loved
me. . . . She pulled me down until I kissed her—
. . . Then she was wise enough to get up and go
to bed; but I kissed her again in the dark after
I had blown out our solitary lamp.

— VITA SACKVILLE-WEST, diary entry on Violet
Trefusis, *Portrait of a Marriage*

Shall I turn and take
comfortless snow within my arms?
press lips to lips
that answer not,
press lips to flesh that shudders not nor breaks?

—H.D., "Fragment Thirty-Six"

We kissed often, our mouths filling up with
tongue and teeth and spit and blood where I bit
her lower lip, and with my hands I held her
against my hip bone.

—JEANETTE WINTERSON, *Sexing the Cherry*

SEX & DESIRE

I am being led I am being led I am being
    gently led to bed
I am being led I am being led, I am being
    gently led.

—GERTRUDE STEIN, "Didn't Nelly and Lilly Love
                    You"

~

Sexual tension can be a gift, if we think of it
that way. It means we are alive, vibrant, aware,
sexual.

—JUDITH MCDANIEL, *The Lesbian Couples' Guide*

~

I want you more than ever for my very, very
own, for always. It is quite beyond my control.

—VIOLET TREFUSIS, letter to Vita Sackville-West,
                Portrait of a Marriage

Rule out especially sexual love, which occupies so much of our public and private thought. Which, despite the plethora of information about it, repeatedly leads us into unwise coupling, unhappy breakups, and increases in an over-stretched population. Of course, sexual love seems colossal, the orchestra is playing full blast and suddenly you discover you move like Fred Astaire.

—BIA LOWE, *Pet, Noun and Verb*

We met at Art School on a shiny corridor. She came towards me so swiftly that the linoleum dissolved under her feet. I thought, "A woman who can do that to an oil cloth can certainly do something for me."

—JEANETTE WINTERSON, *The Poetics of Sex*

＊

"Frenchy," Edie said wondrously, digging her fingers into her shoulders. "I don't know why it took me so long to do this," she whispered.

"To come out?"

"Is that what you call it?" Edie asked between kisses.

"Yeah," Frenchy said, "and this is how you do it." Her hand reached under Edie's nylon panties.

—LEE LYNCH, *The Swashbuckler*

＊

"I've brought you a sweet, you greedy little thing," she said and pulled it out of her bag.

Oh yes, I was greedy, but not for sweets. Her hands were my possession. I covered them with kisses.

"There, there, Olivia," she said. 'You're too passionate, my child."

Her lips brushed my forehead, and she was gone.

—DOROTHY STRACHEY, *Olivia*

The room is filled with the strange scent
of wisteria blossoms.
The sway in the moon's radiance
And tap against the wall.
But the cup of my heart is still,
And cold, and empty.

When you come it brims
Red and trembling with blood.

——AMY LOWELL, "Absence"

The ladies had one common bed that night,
Their bed the same but different their repose.
One sleeps, one moans and weeps in piteous
    plight
Because her wild desire more fiercely glows.

——ARIOSTO, *Orlando Furioso* (1531)

Thou hast with thy Alinda a friend, who will
be a faithfull copartner of all thy misfortunes,
who hath left her father to follow thee and
chooseth rather to brooke all extremities than
to forsake thy prescence. . . . As we have been
bedfellowes in royalitie, we shall be fellowe mates
in pouvertie: I will ever bee thy Alinda, and thou
shalt ever rest to me Rosalynde; so shall the world
canonize our friendship and speak of Rosalynde
and Alinda; as they did of Pilades and Orestes.

—THOMAS LODGE, *Rosalynde*

Yet, sometimes, going about the house, in passing each other, they would fall into an agonized
embrace, looking into each other's face, their two
heads in their four hands, so strained together
that the space that divided them seemed to be
thrusting them apart.

—DJUNA BARNES, *Nightwood*

How can I ever grow accustomed to the beauty of your cheek against my breast or the protective strength with which you turn me over? How can I ever think it ordinary, your desire to caress the tighter places, to take the time to calm me and then to help me want what I cannot see? Or how you reach for me after I have pleasured, pulling me up along your body, your fingers gently cleaning my lips that glisten with your taste? Or how you make a pillow of your shoulder, to comfort me after the coming?

—JOAN NESTLE, *The Gift of Touch*

Your [*sic*] not the only woman who has ever been desired in the world. And you certainly won't be the last, but no woman could have possibly been more desired than you are.

—RADCLYFFE HALL, letter to Lady Una Troubridge

Truly, my sweet love
I do not exaggerate:
Without you, even my own speech
Seems foreign to me.

For the wanting of you
Exceeds all the torture
That cruelty abbetted by skill
Could invent.

—SOR JUANA INES DE LA CRUZ, "Happy Easter,
My Lady"

It is not sensuality that ensures the fidelity of two
women but a kind of blood kinship. . . . I have
written kinship where I should have said identity.
Their close resemblance guarantees similarity in
volupté. The lover takes courage in her certainty of
caressing a body whose secrets she knows, whose
preferences her own body has taught her.

—COLETTE, *Ces Plaisirs*

I want you so much. I long for you. Nay, I cannot do without you; so at all events, you must come. . . . You shall dine, sup and sleep with me alone. I will have you all to myself.

—"Sophie to Jessica," an unpublished fragment by CHARLES BROCKDEN BROWN, from *Surpassing the Love of Men*

I wonder can it really be that you
And I are here alone, and that the night
Is full of hours, and all the world asleep,
And none to call to you to come away;
For you have given all yourself to me,
Making me gentle by your willingness.

—AMY LOWELL, "Dipsa"

She cried Laura, up the garden,
Did you miss me?
Come and kiss me.
Never mind my bruises,
Hug me, kiss me, suck my juices
Squeezed from goblin fruits for you,
Goblin pulp and goblin dew.
Eat me, drink me, love me;
Laura, make much of me . . .

—CHRISTINA ROSSETTI, "Goblin Market"

They do not know, those who enter here, that
every night the weight of our two united bodies
hollows out a little more, beneath its voluptuous
winding sheet, that valley no wider than a tomb.

—COLETTE, *Nuit Blanches*

"I live in the desert of the heart," Evelyn said quietly.

"I can't love the whole damned world."

"Love me, Evelyn."

"I do."

"But you don't want me?"

Evelyn looked at Ann, the child she had always wanted, the friend she had once had, the lover she had never considered. Of course she wanted Ann.

—JANE RULE, *Desert of the Heart*

When they walked together, Lillian sometimes asked Djuna: 'Walk in front of me, so I can see how you walk. You have such a sway of the hips!'

—ANAÏS NIN, *Cities of the Interior*

Manke: . . . you're my bride and I'm your bride-groom. We embrace. . . . We're pressed together and we kiss very quietly, like this. . . . We blush, we're so embarrased. It's good, isn't it Rivkele?

Rivkele: Yes, Manke, it is.

Manke: . . . And then we go to sleep in the same bed. No one sees us, no one knows, just the two of us, like this. . . . Would you like to sleep the whole night through with me, Rivkele, in the same bed?

Rivkele: I would, I would.

Manke: Come, Come.

—SHOLOM ASCH, *The Gods of Vengenance*

Life is all about seduction and great fucking.

—SANDRA BERNHARD, *Love, Love and Love*

What had happened to them last night was something beyond their control. Then let this strange force follow its own law—let it part them forever or join them forever. It was something too big for their reason, and too delicate . . . of no use to fight, reason or wonder.

—ANTHONY THORNE, *Delay of the Sun*

I lay on my back, one arm under her as she, on her side, snuggled her head into my shoulder and fitted her body to mine. I held her close, one hand in her fine hair, one hand on her back, my lips against her forehead. She murmured, I feel like I've waited my whole life to be held like this. I, too, had waited my whole life to hold someone like this. We had found each other, and our love that had lasted through centuries had blossomed again.

—SKY VANDERLINDE, *Loving Blue*

Turn down to me your eyes, so blue and full
of stars!
For just one charming glance, divinely healing
balm,
I'll raise the veil for you of pleasure's secret
depths,
And lull you fast asleep within an endless
dream!

—CHARLES BAUDELAIRE, "Condemned Women:
Delphine and Hippolyta"

a long time lo(u)nging our bodies two-gether to
pass under cover of the night. Mad and incompat-
ible like two aborted heterosexuals who cannot
penetrate each other. The scar must form. I put
my mouth with your sex. Inner saliva. Eat and
think as though there were no end.

—NICOLE BROSSARD, *These Our Mothers: Or the
Disintegrating Chapter*

—

... I was yours, yours to bend over and kiss when the fancy seized you. And sometimes we loved each other so much that we became inarticulate, content only to probe each other's eyes for the secret that was a secret no longer.

—VIOLET TREFUSIS, letter to Vita Sackville-West, *Portrait of a Marriage*

—

We are sixteen. . . .

She is naked. Like Lady Godiva's, her long chestnut hair hides her breasts. I brush the hair away and begin the night's ritual. But tonight is different. I have never tasted a woman and so this night will be special. She bites my neck, my ears, and comes in my mouth.

—CHEA VILLANUEVA, *In the Shadows of Love*

She put her hands on Cécilé's bare arms and as she twisted her round, bent down and kissed her shoulder. A long deliberate kiss on the naked creamy shoulder. An unknown pang of astonishing violence stabbed me. I hated Cécilé.

—DOROTHY STRACHEY, *Olivia*

She lit a candle on an enamel bracket. The light filled the room with darkness. Like a sleeping child she slipped out of her frock and then, suddenly, turned to me and flung her arms round my neck. Every bird upon the bulging frieze broke into song. Every rose upon the tattered paper budded and formed into blossoms. Yes, even the green vine upon the bed curtains wreathed itself into strange chaplets and garlands, twined round us in a leafy embrace, held us with a thousand clinging tendrils.
And Youth was not dead.

—KATHERINE MANSFIELD, *Leves Amores*

Ever since that night I have been a new crea-
ture;to be locked in your arms; to share your
pillowwith you, gave new force, new existence to
the love which before united us; often shall we
pass such nights when thou and I are safe
together . . .

— "Jessica to Sophie," an unpublished fragment
by CHARLES BROCKEN BROWN, from *Surpassing
the Love of Men*

The sadness of our weary lovemaking, night
Comes like the pain of parting
Comes like the poems that don't move us
      anymore
Passes like the black imperial march
The dark sounds of torches towards
      evening . . .

— RENÉE VIVIEN, "Sad Words"

Veronica dropped her robe to the floor and began to stroke her naked self against velvet Samaria. She pulled the wrapping from Samaria's head; she unfastened the comb and hairpins from Samaria's hair.

"If I called you by other names sometimes and the names sounded real enough," she whispered, "would you answer to them?"

"I am willing to listen," said Samaria.

—BERTHA HARRIS, *Lover*

Sex slaves are full of surprises. They combine magic tricks with good politics. Some people can open beer bottles with their mouths; Y unsnaps my bra with her teeth while whistling a politically correct song about Nicaragua.

—CARMELITA TROPICANA, speech at the L.U.S.T. Conference

Your beauty drowns me, drowns the core of me. When your beauty burns me I dissolve as I never dissolved before man. . . . I see in you that part of me which is you. I feel you in me; I feel my own voice becoming heavier, as if I were drinking you in, every delicate thread of resemblance being soldered by fire and one no longer detects the fissure.

—ANAÏS NIN, *The House of Incest*

Oh, come, sweet flock of girls!
I want to drink of your beauty.
Give your wild hair to the wind,
and drop your raiments
silently.

—MARIE-MADELEINE, "Sappho"

—

How slender your young limbs are,
and how childish your budlike breasts!
But in your eyes, my blonde child,
burn the torches of wild lust.

　　　—MARIE-MADELEINE, "Crucifixia"

—

I break wild roses, scatter them over her.
The thorns between us sting like love's pain.
Her flesh, bitter and salt to my tongue,
I taste with endless kisses and taste again.

　—ELSA GIDLOW, "For the Goddess Too Well
　　　　　　Known"

LOVE WITH AN ATTITUDE

. . . For, let her
run, she will soon run after;
if she won't accept gifts, she
will one day give them; and if
she won't love you—she soon will
love, although unwillingly. . . .

—SAPPHO, "Prayer to my Lady of Paphos"

Frenchy smiled, a large winning smile, and
leaned back against the plate glass window,
hooking her thumbs in her belt. She mused,
"That's how I like it, Jess, light. A new girl
every few weeks would suit me fine."

Jessie poked her with her elbow, chuckling
and nodding. "That's you, Frenchy."

—LEE LYNCH, *The Swashbuckler*

—

"Realistically, how are you ever going to pull it off with a straight woman?"

"But I love her."

"So you can love someone else who's not going to make you feel like a freak. Get a lover who likes being gay and you'll be a lot happier."

"What is this, *West Side Story*? I feel like you're telling me not to date one of the Sharks. She loves me."

—SARAH SCHULMAN, *People in Trouble*

—

You're lucky you're handsome and I'm in love. Otherwise, I wouldn't bother.

—PAT CALIFIA, "A Dash of Vanilla"

ABSENCE

There is no aspect of a relationship that we absolutely have to do together. Each couple will find those areas that join them and those areas that allow them to be special, unique, and exciting to one another.

—JUDITH MCDANIEL, *The Lesbian Couples' Guide*

While we are both in this world there is hope—and surely, surely, we shall meet again. It is as though I struck the rock with the staff of my love and at last the spring gushed out, out of your heart into mine, beloved.

—RADCLYFFE HALL, letter to Lady Una Troubridge

Estranged from all, and rapt, I only ask
To be alone when I am not with you

—VITA SACKVILLE-WEST, from "King's Daughter"

There is nothing here in your absence BUT you, more even than when you were here. Everything that happens . . . is but a description of your absence because it is not the same as when you were here. Don't worry that I do not miss you. This place and my life and happiness are like properties with a large cruel sign, For Rent; Unoccupied; Owner gone away . . .

—JANET FLANNER, letter to Natalia Danesi Murray, *Darlinghissima*

"I don't want to leave you," I whispered.

"You're not leaving me. My heart goes with you, just I must stay here."

"Then . . . Maybe you'll write to me. Maybe you'll come back too."

I started to speak but she quieted me.

"Don't make promises now, girl. We make love."

—JEWELLE GOMEZ, *Piece of Fine*

That night Martha waited in her lady's room, just as she used to ... the long years seemed like days. At last she lingered a moment trying to think of something else that might be done, then she was going silently away, but Helena called her back. . . .

"Oh, my dear Martha!" she cried, "Won't you kiss me good night? Oh, Martha, have you remembered like this, all these long years!"

—SARAH ORNE JEWETT, *Martha's Lady*

Ellen, I wish I could live with you always, I begin to cling to you more fondly than I ever did. If we had a cottage and a competency of our own I do think we might love until Death without being dependent on any third person for happiness.

—CHARLOTTE BRONTË, letter to Ellen Nussey

Habit is the anchor of half the love in this world, and my habit of loving her survived the love— or held it, perhaps—for I missed her sorrowfully.

—ROSE TERRY, *My Visitation*

... so for me there is no end. Only I can't, I can't wait forever! ... I can't live without my heart!

—DJUNA BARNES, *Nightwood*

I miss you and wish I were you yourself, sometimes, so I could understand you, thus understanding me and could finally find peace.

—JANET FLANNER to Natalia Danesi Murray, *Darlinghissima*

Remote, unfriended, melancholy, slow
Where mountains rise, and where rude waters
    flow,
Where e'er I go, what ever realms I see,
My heart untravelled fondly turns to thee.
Still to my Fanny turns, with ceaseless pain,
And drags at each remove a lengthening chain.

—ANONYMOUS, "The History of Lady Barton,"
    from *Surpassing the Love of Men*

I have examined and do find,
    of all that favour me,
There is none I grieve to leave behind
    But only, only thee.
To part with thee I needs must die
    Could parting separate thee and I.

—KATHERINE FOWLER PHILLIPS, "To Mrs. M. A.
    at Parting"

I think about looking at you from across the tables, wanting to reach out and hold your face in my hands wishing you were just like my dreams, soft, forgiving, the characteristics I long to impose on you—how can anyone live up to them?

—SANDRA BERNHARD, *Love, Love and Love*

I won't say what I went through during the six weeks that passed before I saw her again. I seemed to know every variety of torment—that of longing and aching miserably for someone in whom I had lost faith, that of loving to desparation someone in whose worth I no longer believed.

—VITA SACKVILLE-WEST, diary entry, *Portrait of a Marriage*

LOSS

In the resurrection, when we come up looking backward at each other, I shall know you only of all that company. My ears shall turn in the socket of my head; my eyeballs loosened where I am the whirlwind about that cashed expense, my foot stubborn on the cast of your grave.

—DJUNA BARNES, *Nightwood*

"You are my sweetheart," she says, "and if you leave me, you will spend all your life coming back to me." With her tongue and her words and the quiet movement of her hand over my skin, she has drawn for me all the limits of my life, and of my love. It is the one love that has created me and will contain me, and if she left me I'd be lonely, and I'd rather sleep in the streets with her hand between my legs forever than be lonely.

—BETH NUGENT, *City of Boys*

When I said I'd give my right arm for you, I
    didn't think you'd ask for it, but you did.
You said, Give it to me.
And I said OK.

—REBECCA BROWN, *Forgiveness*

"Do you believe spirits can see those they used
to love?"

"Oh, God knows, my darling, I cannot tell
you. You will be happy, however it is!"

"Do you think so?" she answered, dreamily. "I
have always been a kind of pagan, and I don't—
feel—quite—certain."

—ALICE FRENCH, *My Lorelei*

For it has been by tenderness
    Already so much bruis'd
Then at your Altars I may guess
    It will be but refus'd
For never Deity did prize
A torn and maimed Sacrifice.

—KATHERINE FOWLER PHILIPS, "To the Lady E.
                Boyle" (1664)

. . . before I die I want to see
The world that lies behind the strangeness of
    your eyes

—CHARLOTTE MEW, "On the Road to the Sea"

Dead is dead but that is why memory is all and
all the immortality there is.

—ALICE B. TOKLAS

Karin: But we talked about it earlier, we always want to be honest with each other. But you can't bear it. You'd prefer me to tell lies.

Petra: Yes, lie to me. Please lie to me.

Karin: All right, it's not true. I was out walking by myself all night and thinking about us.

Petra: Yes? (hopefully) That's not true?

Karin: Of course not . . .

—RAINER WERNER FASSBINDER, *The Bitter Tears of Petra von Kant* (film)

O! when we meet, (to meet we're destin'd, try
    To avoid it as thou may'st) on either brow,
    Nor in the stealing conciousness of eye,
Be seen the slightest trace of what, or how
    We once were to each other; nor one
    sigh
Flatter with Weak regret a broken vow!

—ANNA SEWARD, "Sonnet XIX: To————"

You are going to leave me; and, too, probably forever. . . . All that now remains of the friendship, which was the pride and happiness of my life, will be the sad remembrance of a good I once enjoyed, and which is fled forever! . . . How shall I teach my heart to forget you! How shall I bear the conversation of other young women of our age and condition, after being used to yours! . . . I was happy, and I am so no more. I must lose you! There is no remedy! Tears efface my letters as I write!

—CHARLOTTE LENNOX, *Euphemia*

Be to her, Persephone,
All the things I might not be;
Take her head upon your knee.
She that was so proud and wild
Flippant, arrogant and free,
She that had no need of me.

—EDNA ST. VINCENT MILLAY, "Memorial to D. C."

You fall in love. You're young, inexperienced. What the hell, maybe you're a virgin, even. You fall, up to your ears, and there's nobody to talk to, nobody to lean on. You're all alone with that great big miserable feeling and she's driving you out of your mind. Every time you look at her, every time you're near her. Finally you give into it . . . and she's straight.

—ANN BANNON, *I Am a Woman*

Too late we met. The burning brain,
The aching heart alone can tell
How filled our souls with death and pain
When came the last said word, Farewell!

—ADAH ISAACS MENKEN, "A Memory; To a
Dead Woman"

In passed times I think there hath been none
In time to come it will not be believed,
That love should make by such a strong
        infection
One woman beare another such affection

        —ARIOSTO, *Orlando Furioso*

No one can ever fall so far without breaking her
heart.

        —SANDRA BERNHARD, *Love, Love and Love*

now I know
beginning and end are one
and slay each other

        —MAY SWENSON, "You Are"

Yet at your feet while thus I lye,
  And languish by your Eyes,
Tis far more glorious here to dye,
  Than gain another Prize
Here let me sigh, her let me gaze,
  And wish at least to find
As raptur'd nights, and tender days,
  As he to who you're kind.

—APHRA BEHN, "A Song, by Mrs. A.B."

The gods bless you
May you sleep then
on some tender
girl friend's breast

—SAPPHO, "The gods bless you"

Now Emmaline was no longer worthy of her passion. Was her own life wrong? Must one be like such clods to be happy? Should she have four children? . . . No! She repudiated such spineless notions. She was what she was. She thrust from her her old dream of Emmaline's breast, she jeered at Emmaline's bovine happiness.

—CATULLE MENDES, *Méphistophélia*

If you love someone very much and they want to destroy you, that is enough to destroy you.

—SARAH SCHULMAN, *People in Trouble*

I am nothing but the memory of her.

—ALICE B. TOKLAS (letter)

DECLARATIONS/

DECLAMATIONS

Thus I pray you, if it please you that true love
and celebration and sweet humility
should bring me such relief with you,
if it please you, lovely woman, then give me
that which most hope and joy promises,
for in you lie my desire and my heart
and from you stems all my happiness,
and because of you I'm often sighing

—BIERIS DE ROMANS, from *Surpassing the Love of
Men*

Think not 'tis needless to repeat desires;
The fervent turtles alwaies court and bill,
And yet their spotless passion never tires,
But does increase by repetition still. . . .

—KATHERINE FOWLER PHILLIPS, "To My
Lucasias, in Defense of Declared Friendship"

[I]f she was kind in speech or act—if she spoke to me caressingly—if she put her warm lips upon my cheek—I was thrilled with joy; her presence affected me, as sunshine does, with a sense of warm life and delight; when we rode, walked or talked together, I wished the hour eternal; and when she fell into some passion, and burned me with bitter words, stinging me into retort by their injustice, their hard cruelty, it was I who repented—I who humiliated myself—I who, with abundant tears, asked her pardon, worked, plead, prayed to obtain it; and if some spasmodic conscientiousness rousted her to excuse herself— to say that she had been wrong—my hands closed her lips: I could not hear that: the fault was mine, mine only. I was glad to be the clay as long as she was queen and deity.

—ROSE TERRY, *My Visitation*

You are the landmark that leads me through the streets of the everyday. You take me past the little houses towards the church where we worship. . . . I miss the weals of our passion just as I miss the daily tenderness of choosing you. Choosing you above all others, my pearl of great price.

—JEANETTE WINTERSON, *The Poetics of Sex*

I like her & being with her, & the splendour—she shines . . . with a candle-lit radiance, stalking on legs like beech trees, pink glowing, grape clustered, pearl hung.

—VIRGINIA WOOLF, diary entry about Vita Sackville-West

I parade through my life for you. My past life, so rational and rationalized now, is open to your gaze. Of course, you will see things about me that I will never see, others will never see. You will know things about me that words cannot capture, that you cannot tell me. Your gaze is of the cruel scientist about to dissect. And I am still drawn in, like a rat caught in the cobra's gaze. A tantalizing split second from death, frozen in the lover's embrace that becomes a strangulation.

—BARBARA SMITH, *Exercising Restraint*

I'm so bad for you but I need the refuge of your perfect arms to hold me when I feel for certain that I might be going insane.

—SANDRA BERNHARD, *Love, Love and Love*

Speak to me tenderly,
think of me lovingly.
Let your soft hands smooth back my hair. . . .
Let my lonely life creep into your warm bosom,
    knowing
no other rest than this

—ADAH ISAACS MENKEN, "Answer Me"

"For you alone I reserve that Gasp under Gasp,
that Sigh behind Sigh, that Attention back of
feigned; that Cloud's Silver is yours—take it! What
care have I on whom it rains! The real me is your
real yours, I can spend myself in Hedgerow and
Counter-patch, 'tis only the Dust of my reality,
the Smoke that tells of the fire, which my own
Darling Lamb, my most perfect and tirelessly different, is yours, I am thine! You compel me!"

—DJUNA BARNES, *Ladies Almanack*